Vol. II

Where Are We?

Remember Me!

By:

Devon St. Laurent

www.aaronpublishing.com

Printed in the United States of America

First Printing, June 2018

ISBN 978-1-7324444-0-9

Published by

Aaron Publishing

PO Box 1144

Shelbyville, TN 37162

This sequel of "Where Are We?" is a foundational book. Remember Me, Volume II is designed to rebuild and strengthen your relationship and walk with Jesus Christ. Once you have read this book, there is a sinner's prayer for you to read. Your decision is ultimately your decision. Whether you choose to walk and convert your life over to Christ is between you and Him. I promise you won't regret it and the rewards are more than you could possibly fathom. After finishing these books I pray you will choose Heaven and not Hell as your eternal home and gain an understanding that both are more real than you might have once believed.

Table of Contents

Remember Me

God never said that life would be easy. Sometimes we have to go through trials we wish we never experienced or even have to encounter, but those are the trials that truly make us who we are.

When we overcome, we become VICTORS instead of keeping a mentality that we are a VICTIM.

Satan only comes to steal, kill, and destroy. So why do we make it so easy for him to enter in? We only fall in life when we allow him to enter in through, anger, stress, depression, etc… Satan uses those cracked doors to lodge a wedge between us and God. Those are avenues in which he gains influence over us in order to control us. But we RISE because we know we are not weak, that we are indeed strong.

We are only human. Yes, we make mistakes, but it's those mistakes in life that build us up stronger. God said, *"I will never give you more than you can bear."* (1 Corinthians 10:13)

When we hit rock bottom and nothing seems to be going our way, our first mistake is to blame God. Never blame God for something negative that happens in your life. Instead of blaming God when you hit rock bottom, embrace him and always praise him, because it's really not God's fault. Believe it or not, it's not Satan's fault either. God created us with the freedom to make our own choices, in other words, we are given a free-will. God doesn't mess with free-will; he just influences you to make right choices. Satan has no power over free-will; he just influences us to make wrong choices.

God never wills for anything bad to happen, but he can allow us to hit rock bottom, just to remind us and prove a point. He has a hilarious sense of humor. He allows us to hit rock bottom to remind us that HE IS the rock at the bottom. God wants to always re-establish new foundations for us before raising us up again.

Remember, we are only human, we have moments of weakness, but overcoming with Jesus allows you to move from being a VICTIM to a VICTOR. We are not weak because we surrender, we become strong because we admit that we are weak and need a Savior. We are worthy. When Jesus sacrificed his life to save us from our sins and eternal damnation, we became worthy. Our past should not be an embarrassing scar we don't want anyone to see or know about.

You're building stronger testimonies to reach those WHO ARE, ARE ABOUT TO, or WHO HAVE ALREADY gone through what you went through or are going through.

It's your testimony that becomes your ordination to minister to those who need help regarding decisions made or about to be made that will lead them away from Christ and their salvation.

For those who claim not to have gone through such turmoil, they should consider themselves blessed that God kept them away from things He obviously felt they couldn't handle especially on their own. He kept them hidden under the rock. But they must not make themselves out to be holier than thou just because they haven't had a traumatic past. It only creates hypocrisy.

Never look down on someone unless you are helping them up, for no one is without blemish. For we all have sinned and fallen short of the Glory of God. How much grace has God shown you? Don't you think you should show the same grace and love he has shown you?

I want God to say to me, "Well done my good and faithful servant, not, I don't know you," and that should scare and worry you. Fear God, not man. He said follow me, not man.

False Christians walk among the true, unfortunately. Those who are lost, trust me they know God, and they know John 3:16, but it's not circumstances in life that draw them away from God, it FALSE CHRISTIANS that lead them astray. What I mean about false Christians, is that they act one way in church and then act a completely different way outside of the church and most of the time have to question if they have any idea what it means to be a Christian at all. It can make someone a hypocrite and it draws those away who need God because they see Christians, but they don't see Christ in them.

Just because someone sins or has sinned differently than us, doesn't make them any less of a person than us, for God is no respecter of persons. His Love *will* endure forever.

Christ died as a sacrifice for all mankind. He saved us from our sins that nailed him to a tree. He took on sin; the burden of the world, so that one day we might be free and experience peace, love, and happiness. I was lost and confused at one point when depression and anger had taken over. With death on my mind at more than one point, feeling like there was nothing left for me, my life felt like it was being devoured. At times it seemed as if there was no hope, I had no positive point of view. My life felt incomplete, until that day when I found Jesus.

I had him before, but I didn't know him. I just knew of him. I was spring cleaning my house as they say and I came across a book that had hardly been used and had so much dust you couldn't read the cover. I grabbed it and immediately heard such a beautiful voice. I answered to hear more, I wanted to hear Jesus. I was lost and I had a one-on-one, slap in the face of the reality that brought me to my knees in an empty car lane and He let know who He was and why He loved me, even though most of the time I couldn't bear to love myself.

This is what Jesus said to me…

Come to me my child, come and I shall give you rest. I see you troubled and weary. Take the book that lies in your hands, read and you will never grow hungry. I love you, my child. Wipe the tears that fall on your cheeks, you have been healed, you are redeemed.

Hello

Hello, my name is Jesus, and I would like to introduce myself.

I came to Earth to endure a life that you must live, a life that was never meant for you, a life that was never intended for you.

Your ancestors, Adam and Eve, fell from grace when they allowed Satan to persuade them to sin against me. Satan transformed himself into a serpent and with cunning cleverness he used and twisted his words to convince Eve to sin.

When I was walking with Eve in the Garden I told her not to eat of the forbidden tree and Satan used that to open the door to sin through desirable temptation. Satan knows the Bible from cover to cover because he was once an Angel in Heaven with me. Satan fell from grace when he decided to challenge my Father. He was sentenced to Hell and therefore Hell was created for those who choose to set themselves against God.

Eve along with Adam both ate of the forbidden tree and they both fell from grace. After they ate of the tree of knowledge they both saw that they were naked and hid from each other, made clothes out of the resources around them, and shielded themselves away from me because they knew they had sinned.

Adam and Eve tried to hide from me, but I already knew what they had done. The Garden became cursed. It dried up, died, and thorns took over the area. They had to live with their mistake and their consequence was to live a cursed life, a life that meant they were no longer a perfect creation and the bridge between God and themselves had been broken.

I decided to do something about it. My Father knows the times of the seasons and He has his own timing. I knew I would have to wait for the right time to intervene, a time when it was my turn. I would have to wait for a heart of gold, a heart unblemished by the world and ways around her, a woman that was full mine—body, and soul, devoted to my Father. I had to wait for Mary.

I knew that I had to do something to save my brothers and sisters. My Father and I discussed that a sacrifice had to be made. A lamb perfect without sin or blemish of any kind had to be given, then broken, blessed and then taken for there to be saving peace and new promises made, allowing the New Testament to be written.

My Father was a little hesitant of course, but then again what Father wouldn't be, knowing his son would have to suffer in the worst brutal way. The crucial importance of the suffering eased any discomfort that I may have had and allowed me to love more than any human could and even understand the depth of the word.

It was time to go about my Father's business. I left my earthly Father's home and went on my way. There was quite a bit of road to walk and miracles to perform so I am only going to touch base on a couple of them. I wanted to rekindle a lost flame in my people that Satan tried to destroy. The main purpose in my three years was to provide not only hope but the foundation they needed to claim Heaven and break Hell.

Your main purpose in life is to finish my journey and continue what I started—that is to preach my Father's words and reach the ends of the Earth until His truth reached every knick and cranny. Once this has come to pass, then shall I hear from my Father, forgive your sins and transgressions and heal your land.

One of the men I met was Peter. Peter was one of my followers and a true friend and believer in me. One night while on the water, a storm came while he and his men were fishing and it was a storm that would truly test not only his patience but a storm that would test his faith in me.

I was watching from a distance and all I could hear was fear, worry, and disappointment. They were crying out to me so I appeared. I started walking toward them on the water and called out to Peter. I called out to him to walk out to me. At first, he was hesitant and wanted to argue, but I called out to him, "Peter, come to me!"

Peter straddled the side of the boat and began walking on the water towards me. All he had to do was keep his eyes on me and have faith that he could reach me. He took his eyes off of me and began to sink into the water. I reached out my hand to him.

"Ye of little faith, Peter take my hand." I had to teach Peter that as long as he keeps me first, has faith in me, and trusts me, he had nothing to worry about, that I would always be there. All you need is faith the size of a grain of mustard seed to move mountains.

Along in my journey, I came across a woman that was well-known among the men. Her name was Mary Magdalene. I had a lesson to teach not only her but to all the men that showed up to stone her. This lesson would teach, grace and mercy, and words from my Father would pierce their hearts helping them acknowledge their own sins.

I walked over to the woman and immediately interjected. Before the first man could throw the first stone I stood in front of her, turned towards the crowd and said, "Let He who is without sin cast the first stone." It reminds me of what my Father said, "Surely your sins will find you out." I started drawing in the dirt and one by one they all walked away.

For you have all sinned and come short of the glory of my Father. No sin is too big or too small for me to forgive. I love you and I want a relationship with you. I have shown you and will continue to show you my love, grace, and mercy just like I showed that woman. I am not saying to sin and I'll forgive you every time, I'm saying to go and sin no more.

No matter what you have done or are going to do, remember that I know and understand because I had to live it as well so I could understand and acknowledge your sufferings. I forgive you and I love you.

I came along on my journey and reached its pinnacle end. I was so full of love that it helped me when I was carrying my cross. I was whipped and beaten. I suffered to save you and heal you. I was nailed to the cross and pleaded with my Father to forgive you for you knew not what you were doing.

I hung there until it was my time and on the exact time I spoke, "It is finished." I bore the sins of the world so that I could enter Hell and claim back the keys from Satan. My body was taken off the cross and placed in a tomb. I rose on the third day to finish the prophecy that was being written and carried out and joined my Father on his right hand to be an intercessor for you.

A new bridge has been created to take the place of the one that fell from the demise of Adam and Eve so that you can have a new relationship with your Father like I have with him. I will always be with you and I will never leave you nor will I ever forsake you. REMEMBER ME!

My Purpose—Jesus

Jesus spoke to me in my hour of deepest need when I was almost on my way out, "Spiritually." I didn't know what to do, say, or anything. But just when I almost forgot who I was in Christ and almost forgot who Jesus was to me, Jesus reminded me and this is what He said to me. NOW, Let Him Speak To You…

I came to Earth to endure the life that you must live. I overcame sin, the World, and Hell, so that I may know and feel your pain.

I came as a human like you, so that I may understand your strengths and weaknesses. I came to save you from sin and eminent Hell so that you may have life and have it more abundantly.

I wanted the curse to be lifted off of you so that you may be free and have a home with me in Heaven. My burden is light and my yoke is easy. Please let go of yours, drop it at my feet, leave it there and don't look back or pick it up.

You have scars that needed healing, so my body was whipped and scarred to heal you from yours. The Garden was cursed with thorns after the fall of man from eating of the forbidden tree, so I wore a crown of thorns upon my head to uplift the curse.

My blood was shed so that yours may be cleansed of all unrighteousness and become as white as snow. Though your sins are as red as crimson, you are now washed in the blood of the Lamb, cleansed and forgiven of your sins. I was placed upon a Dogwood cross to bear the sins of the World. I set a reminder in the pedal blooms of the Dogwood tree of a drop of blood at the tips to remind those of my sacrifice.

I entered the gates of Hell to reclaim back possession of the keys so that the gates of Hell we never prevail against you and be locked to those who believe in me and submit entirely to me.

I rose on the third day to restore my covenant with you and rebuilt a bridge that never should have been broken.

With my death, may you die too and rise from the ashes like a phoenix and live forever with me. I died to save you, heal you, and one day, bring you home.

Take of my bread and remember my body which was broken for you, that you may be healed and forgiven of your sins, transgressions, and iniquities.

Take of the cup and remember my blood that was shed for you to wash and cleanse you from all unrighteousness. Do this in remembrance of me. Live a holy life and be ready for my return.

Praise God and AMEN…

My Purpose For You

Why are we here? What is our purpose? What is your purpose? Each one is different. We are not here by chance; we are here with a purpose and with meaning. We are not here just for ourselves. Like a breeze on a hot day. Like trees that feed on the sunlight.

There is a reason for everything; everything has its place: PURPOSE. God never intended for us to work for a living at a job. He never intended for money to be our air to breathe here on Earth. Unfortunately, that is just a part of the curse from Adam and Eve we have to deal with because sin was brought into the world. It's our job, duty, and purpose to ease the burden and help carry each others, which is why I am writing this.

The burden of others should be ours; it should be yours. When you see a need, fill a need. We are to SHOW Jesus and BE Jesus to those who NEED Him and to those who are WITHOUT him. It SHOULD be our priority and problem when we see someone hurting, lost, and in need.

We should WANT to help and we SHOULD help because that is the whole point of being a Christian. Take the "ian" out of

"Christian" and that's what you should be showing others, "Christ." There is no reason for you to be so caught up in yourself that you wonder what it will do TO you or FOR you because it's not about YOU. If it was, Jesus would have only sacrificed his life for you and only you but he didn't. He sacrificed his life for the world and everyone it. God said He will take care of us and supply all of our needs according to his riches and glory, but until we get it through our thick skull that it means doing God's work and spreading his love and the Gospel of Christ, we won't see it, because we won't be showing him that we've earned it.

Ask yourself these questions:

1) How many people have I won to the Lord?

2) Have I stayed in contact with them to show them and prove to them that I really do care not only about them as a person but about their salvation to take part in their inheritance?

3) Do I show Christ with and in everything that I do and say? Have I spread the love and the Gospel of Christ to those in need of it, to those who are lost, and to those who just need a reboot charge of the Holy Ghost Fire?

Let me ask you this.

1) What would you rather hear, "Well done my good and faithful servant" or "Depart from Me, I do not know You," and then be destined for Hell instead of Heaven?

It all comes down to a choice, sooner or later you will have to decide. You can enjoy your life and waste it away never using your life to its fullest potential for the Kingdom of Heaven or you can never make the decision to change your life, accept Jesus as your Lord and personal Savior, and spend eternity in Hell.

Like I said, sooner or later, you will have to choose because I'm here to tell you— both Heaven and Hell are more real than you can possibly fathom and the end is coming quicker than you think.

NOW IS THE TIME. Stop living in a "YOU" world and remember that it's not about you; it's about the lost sheep of the Earth that need the Shepherd. Our mission field doesn't have to be overseas or out of state. It can be as simple as next door to us, the grocery store, or at our job. The point of church is not to be a personal sanctuary for us from the world. It's about getting the teaching, knowledge, coaching, and criticism we need to knock those walls down to share and lead in a dying and decaying world that's bound for Hell.

Be a leader instead of a follower, we have too many followers already. Take action and literally practice what you preach and what is preached to you. Be the lighthouse for lost ships in the night and for people going through their own storms and attract them to your light in order to bring them home to Christ. Don't be comfortable with a pew seat, instead, get restless and uncomfortable and amped up for leaving the walls of the church and share what you know and have learned.

I have two friends who have moved to Hawaii to start their own church, led by God, to reach the islands of Hawaii because over 70% is lost and without God. I'm not saying you need to drop everything, go out, and start a church, but you also don't need to go to school to minister. In my personal opinion, I think that's what keeps a lot of people from taking action because churches stress it and it's completely wrong. GOD ordains people NOT man. You need to reread your Bible if you question that statement. There is no law above God's law.

If you have a calling on your heart and you want to help by putting your faith in action within our broken borders by reaching out to show the love of Christ and spread the Gospel to the lost and broken, then STOP WAITING on man to say yes and listen to God because HE IS saying yes. That is the whole point of being a Christian. It is to show Christ and prove Christ mighty in their lives and your own.

God will always take care of us when we work in HIS purpose that he has for us instead of trying to work on our OWN, whether it's in our neighborhood, out of state or overseas. Don't sacrifice someone's soul and inheritance and lose yours in the process. It may come as an inconvenience because carnal ways of the world cause one to think of themselves other than someone else. We must account on judgment day for everything negative that we, think, say, didn't say, didn't think, do, or didn't do.

Be the light that you are always praying for. Be your OWN miracle and let God work through YOU instead of just waiting for something to happen, that He can do through us.

BE ACTIVE, and only be still when God says so because then he is protecting you from something out of your control and He will move when it's His turn to. OBEDIENCE is your salvation foundation with Christ.

We cannot expect to see a domino effect if we do not act first, whether it be through actual actions or prayer. Ask and we shall receive, if we ask for wisdom He is sure and just to give it to us. No more waiting, because Jesus didn't wait.

Will You Stand?

I will STAND with God and be more than happy to be judged by the world than to STAND with the world and be judged by God. No matter how hard we try and fight the truth, the truth will always find a way to surface to the front. If we deny God, then we will be denied. God is the only Way, the only TRUTH, and the only LIFE; no one comes to the Father but through Him. It's completely up to you, when it comes down to it, it's all a choice. You can either choose to burn in the Lake of Fire in Hell or you can choose to spend eternity in Heaven. Please do not wait until it is too late. Repent and ask God to come into your heart. Get baptized and live your life for God.

Satan vs. Truth—Division Instead of Connection

Satan frames the mind so you believe a false truth. We must remove the blinding veil so we can see with God as our 20/20 sight. So many churches have strayed from Biblical principles and true doctrine just to accommodate the world. If we feel like we have to impress the world we are here for the wrong reasons which will cause sheep to stray.

We are not here to impress or accommodate. We are here to save souls. Jesus didn't say, "Follow Christians," he said, "Follow Me." Most of the time it's Christians that lead the lost astray.

Don't base your feelings and emotions on the ignorance of false Christians. We don't go to church for Christians, we go for a relationship with God and Jesus. Most Christians, unfortunately, need more help than the ones who are lost.

Gossip and clicks are a couple of the top killers of the church and Satan loves every minute of it. Gossip and clicks have divided the church for years; those are the false Christians because they have the high and mighty ego that gives the impression of, "I'm better than your type of personality." Just because we have never had to go through some of the struggles as others, doesn't give us the right to criticize and talk about others behind their back and compare our life to theirs. We are not better than they are, for we have ALL sinned and come short of the glory of God. No sin is greater or less than anyone else's. God is no respecter of persons.

What's more important— a body of tattoos or a wick to their eternal candle that needs to be lit? The things said, not said, things done and not done, and the thoughts we have or had will all have to be accounted for when we reach Heaven. I repeat and stress this because it is so important for us to keep that in your mind. There is no middle with God. It's either, Yay or Nay. Leave YOURSELF out of it and let GOD. We are here to save, not condemn, otherwise we also condemn ourselves. Bless a life not curse it.

I'm tired of churches falling victim to Satan. Unity and love help break the chains of destruction. Stop basing feelings and emotions on Christians and focus only on God because it's about him and not them. Going forward from this point, from the time you read these words let it begin your new year. This is going to be your true due season.

As we await God's return to take us home we must live out our days fully committed to HIS work. The more time we spend building up the Kingdom the more rewards and blessings we shall receive.

If we are not dead, then God is not finished with us yet. He will equip us and if we ask He will grant us the gift of wisdom.

Let's make our new year great. The only thing between us and God is Satan trying to put a wedge. We have the power to close that gap. The closer we get to God the more cunning and clever Satan gets because he doesn't want to lose his hold over us. Prayer is our biggest defense mechanism and if we pray in our prayer language he can hear what we are praying but he can't understand it.

Our prayer language is our secret line straight to God so Satan cannot interfere. We have the power and if we believe with all of our mind, body, and soul, we can defeat anything that Satan tries to throw our way. Amen.

If you would like to know more about prayer language speak to your Pastor or ask an evangelist to guide you through it. Thank you and I hope that this book has and will help you to create a stronger relationship with Christ and a strengthened walk.

Family

I love the family dining room. Dining rooms are meant for family, friends, and fellowship. Do you want to know the beauty of the fact? It doesn't have to be an actual dining room. It could be a car, a living room, picnic tables, etc… whatever, just make sure the TV's and cell phones are turned off and turn on a radio, but just make it a time of personal togetherness.

More and more we see most forgetting what it's like for a family to sit around a dinner table together and eat, talk, and fellowship, and maybe play a game or two after the meal is over. Between the TV's and the cell phones, it's sad how far families have moved apart from each other.

It blows my mind how many families have moved apart from each other. When I see family member's texting each other and having a full blown conversation and they are sitting next to each other, I see a problem and a sad case of, why?

We as a nation need more of God on top and family right underneath. There's a lack of communication in the homes today which causes a lack of love and compassion, therefore causes separation and discord in the home among the family.

I am absolutely truly blessed by the family God has given me, because we still sit around a table together and eat, talk, and fellowship even playing a game together after we are done eating.

This causes joy, love, compassion, and laughter to move in creating a strong bond between each of us to pass on for years to come and eventually allowing me to pass on when I am blessed with children of my own.

I can't express in full just exactly how truly blessed and honored I am to have a family that still believes in being a FAMILY no matter what the world may throw at us. I would rather be judged by the world and stand with God than to stand with the world and be judged by God.

Take my words and let them sink in to renew your relationship with God and Jesus Christ our Lord. Live a full life and pass the love of God on to people that need Him like someone did for you.

Sinner's Prayer

Dear Jesus,

I know that I am a sinner. I believe in you and the Holy Bible. I believe that you came to Earth to save me from my sins. I believe you when you said that I was healed as you bore the sins and ailments of the world upon the cross. I believe you are the Son of God the Father and my Lord and Savior. Thank you, Lord, for my healing and for my Salvation. Please forgive me of my sins, transgressions, and iniquities. I repent of all unrighteousness and ask you to make me whole. Cleanse me and wash me with your blood. Lord Jesus, come into my heart, occupy your home there with your Holy Spirit and fill me with your fire and tongue. I praise you Lord Jesus and give you all the Glory. Baptize me in the name of the Father, the Son, and the Holy Spirit. I pray all this in your Holy and mighty name, Amen.

About the Author

I am a strong believer in Christ Jesus. I was saved in 1997 in Virginia Beach. When I was 14 I lost my spiritual walk with the Lord, gained weight, left church, excluded myself from my family, and even had the thought run through my mind of homosexuality. Moving back to Tennessee, Satan grabbed control and I reached rocked bottom. I became addicted to pain killers and even started smoking and drinking.

I am set free today! I am a life saved! God saw my need, saved me and now I am on the path God had predestined me to take— to save others from making the mistakes that I've made. I have been drug free since 2012 and I refuse to allow Satan to run my life any longer. I went to the enemy's camp and took back what he stole from me and you can too!!!

Contact Devon:

d_saint3@hotmail.com

Other Titles by Devon:

Tornado Boy

Where Are We Vol. I

www.ingramcontent.com/pod-product-compliance
Lightning Source LLC
Chambersburg PA
CBHW060646030426
42337CB00018B/3470

* 9 7 8 1 7 3 2 4 4 4 4 0 9 *